JavaScript

The Ultimate Beginner's Guide!

Andrew Johansen

Table of Contents

Introduction

I want to thank you and congratulate you for getting my book...

"JavaScript: The Ultimate Beginner's Guide!"

This book will help you become an effective JavaScript user. If you want to learn the basics of the JavaScript language quickly and easily, then you must get this book now.

This book will explain important facts regarding the JavaScript language. It doesn't contain any irrelevant information. Each page holds valuable lessons, instructions and examples. After reading this book, you'll be familiar with objects, functions, variables, statements and other JavaScript elements.

Thanks again for purchasing this book, I hope you enjoy it!

CHAPTER 1

General Information

JavaScript is an object-oriented scripting language that you can use in different platforms. Within host environments (e.g. web browsers), you may use JavaScript to gain programmatic control over an object.

This scripting language comes with a rich standard library. This library holds objects (e.g. Math, Date, Array, etc.) and core language elements (e.g. statements, operators, control structures, etc.). As of now, programmers extend JavaScript's basic features by adding extra objects. They do this to improve the language's effectiveness in completing certain tasks.

Here are two of the most popular variants of JavaScript:

- Server-side JavaScript – This variant is designed to help programmers run JavaScript on a web server. For instance, server-side extensions help applications to interact with databases, conduct file changes and provide a continuous flow of information.

- Client-side JavaScript – This form of JavaScript is created for browsers and their respective DOM (i.e. Document Object Model). For instance, client-side JavaScript helps applications to save elements into an HTML document and react to user actions (e.g. form input, mouse clicks, page navigation, etc.).

JavaScript and the Java Language

Java and JavaScript are two different programming languages. JavaScript has some similarities with Java (e.g. naming conventions, expression syntax, control-flow constructs, etc.). However, it doesn't have two of Java's distinctive characteristics: powerful type checking and static typing.

According to many people, these languages are completely unrelated. Netscape (the company who developed JavaScript) changed the name of the language from LiveScript to JavaScript to exploit the popularity enjoyed by Java; thus, the similarity between the names of these languages emerged because of marketing considerations.

At this point, let's discuss the main differences between these programming languages. This piece of information will help you in improving your knowledge about JavaScript and general programming.

JavaScript – This is a free-form computer language. When using JavaScript, you don't have to declare all of the methods, classes and variables. You don't have to worry about the types of methods that you'll use (i.e. whether they are private, public or protected). Additionally, you won't have to implement any interface for JavaScript.

Java – This class-based computer language is created for type safety and quick implementation. This means that you have to use classes and their respective methods to create your

4

programs. Java's data typing and class inheritance require strict object hierarchies. Simply put, the Java language is more complicated than JavaScript.

How to Get Started?

You don't have to download files or install programs into your computer just to use JavaScript. You can simply access your favorite web browser to create your own JavaScript applications. These days, Firefox is one of the best web browsers when it comes to JavaScript programming. Because of that, this book will focus on the tools available in Firefox browsers. If your computer doesn't have Firefox, you are advised to visit this site: https://www.mozilla.org. This browser is free and easy to use; thus, you can easily master the basics of JavaScript without spending any money.

Once you have downloaded Firefox, you'll see two powerful tools created specifically for JavaScript programming. These tools are:

1. Web Console

This tool displays information about the webpage loaded on the screen. It also has a command line feature that you may use to run JavaScript statements on the loaded page.

To access Web Console, you just have to launch Firefox, click on "Tools," and choose "Web Console" from the menu titled "Developer." After activating Web Console, you'll see a command line at the bottom of your screen. You may enter JavaScript expressions into that command line, then the pane at the middle of the screen will show you the results of the expressions you entered.

This feature shows results immediately – you'll quickly know if you have entered codes incorrectly.

Here's a screenshot of the Web Console tool:

2. Scratchpad

Firefox's Web Console is excellent for running single JavaScript expressions. Although you can use it to run multiple lines, you'll find this task extremely inconvenient. Additionally, you can't use that tool to save your code snippets. Fortunately, Firefox has another tool that solves the problems discussed above. This tool is called "Scratchpad."

To access this tool, you have to do the following:

1. Launch the Firefox browser.

2. Click on Tools.

3. Look for the "Developer" section and choose "Scratchpad."

This tool is a separate Firefox window that acts like a text editor. You can use it to write and run JavaScript codes on your browser. Additionally, you may use Scratchpad to save your new codes or load existing ones.

The screenshot below shows an image of the Scratchpad tool:

Your First JavaScript Application

In this section, you'll write your first application using JavaScript. This simple activity will give you a taste of JavaScript's features and programming environment.

Launch Scratchpad and enter the code below:

```
1  function greetMe(yourName) {
2    alert("Hello " + yourName);
3  }
4
5  greetMe("World");
```

Highlight the JavaScript code and press Ctrl+R to see the result on your screen.

The next chapter will discuss the syntax and features of JavaScript; thus, you will be able to create applications that are more complex than the one given above.

CHAPTER 2

The Basic Elements of the JavaScript Language

In this chapter, you'll learn about JavaScript's grammar, variables, data types, and constants/literals.

General Information

The syntax of this programming language is similar to that of Awk, Perl, Java, and Python. Additionally, it is case-sensitive and utilizes Unicode characters.

When using JavaScript, programmers refer to computer instructions as "statements." You should separate statements using a semicolon. JavaScript also supports whitespaces (e.g. tabs, spaces, and newline characters). This means that you may use these characters to improve the readability of your JavaScript statements.

The JavaScript compiler scans source codes from left to right and converts them into groups of input objects (i.e. comments, whitespaces, tokens, line terminators, and control characters).

Comments

JavaScript's syntax for writing comments is similar to that of most programming languages. You must use two slashes (i.e. //)

to create a single-line comment. However, to create a comment that spans multiple lines, you must use /* and */ at the start and end of the comment, respectively. The screenshot below will show you how to use these characters in writing your own codes:

```
1    // a one line comment
2
3    /* this is a longer,
4       multi-line comment
5    */
```

Important Note: JavaScript doesn't support nested comments (i.e. comments placed inside another comment).

The Declarations in JavaScript

The JavaScript programming language supports three types of declarations. These are:

- var – Use this declaration to create a new variable. During the declaration, you may assign a value to the variable.

- let – This declaration allows you to create a local variable. You may place a value on the variable during the declaration phase.

- const – Use this declaration to create a constant. Constants are read-only: you can't change their value after the declaration.

Let's discuss these declarations in detail:

The "var" Declaration

The syntax of this declaration is:

```
var varname1 [= value1 [, varname2 [, varname3 ... [, varnameN]]]];
```

You can replace "varname1" with any valid identifier. JavaScript has reserved keywords – words that cannot be used in naming variables, constants, objects, etc. You'll learn about these keywords later.

In this syntax, "value1" represents the value of the variable. You may replace it with any valid JavaScript expression.

How Does It Work?

The JavaScript interpreter prioritizes variable declarations over any type of code. The variable's scope declared through "var" serves as its active execution context (i.e. either local or global).

If you'll assign a value to a variable that you haven't declared yet, you'll get a global variable (i.e. a variable that can be accessed at any part of your program). Here are the major differences between a declared variable and an undeclared variable:

- A declared variable is limited to the function through which it was declared. That means a function cannot access the declared variables created inside other functions. Undeclared variables, on the other hand, are global 100% of the time.

- JavaScript's interpreter will create declared variables before running any code. Undeclared variables, however, can only exist once the interpreter has run the necessary codes.

- A declared variable is a non-changeable attribute of its respective function. Thus, a function cannot edit or delete the declared variables it contains. Undeclared variables, on the other hand, allow modifications. That means you can edit or delete them, depending on your needs.

Because of the differences outlined above, you'll probably get unexpected or undesirable results from your program if you'll fail to declare variables properly. Thus, it's a good programming behavior to declare variables, regardless of their scope.

The "let" Declaration

Here is the syntax of this declaration:

```
let var1 [= value1] [, var2 [= value2]] [, ..., varN [= valueN]];
```

You may replace "var1" with the name you'd like to use for your variable.

If you want to assign a value to the new variable, just replace "value1" with the appropriate data.

How Does it Work?

This declaration allows you to create variables that are restricted in scope to the expression, block or statement where you used them.

If you'll use "let," the variables that you'll get will consider their container as their scope. In this aspect, "let" is similar to "var." The major difference is that a "var" variable's scope is the whole function that encloses it.

The "const" Declaration

With this declaration, you can create a read-only reference to any value. Basically, you can still edit these references whenever you need to. It's just that you won't be able to transfer or reassign them after the declaration phase. The syntax of this declaration is:

```
const name1 = value1 [, name2 = value2 [, ... [, nameN = valueN]]];
```

How Does It Work?

With this declaration, you can generate a constant (also known as "literal") that can be either local or global. The syntax given above requires an initializer. That means you have to specify the variable's value at the time of declaration.

A constant is block-scoped. In this aspect, constants are similar to variables declared through "let."

Important Note: You cannot change a constant's value through reassignment or "re-declaration."

JavaScript Variables

Variables serve as symbolic identifiers for the values needed by your programs. When naming your variables, you have to remember these rules:

- Start the variable's name using a letter, a dollar sign (i.e. $), or an underscore (i.e. "_"). You may include numbers in the name of your variable. However, you can't start the name using a number. For example: "javascript1" is valid but "1javascript" isn't.

- The JavaScript language is case-sensitive. That means you have to be consistent with letter capitalization when naming variables. For example, JavaScript treats "LETTER," "Letter," "letter" as three different variables.

How to Declare a Variable

In JavaScript, you can declare variables in three different ways:

- Using the "var" keyword - For instance, *var z = 99*. You can use that syntax to create a local or global variable.

- By assigning a value to a non-existing variable - For instance, *z = 99*. This method is much simpler than the previous one. However, you should only use this to create global variables.

- Using the "let" keyword - For instance, *let a = 20*. You can use this syntax to declare block scope variables.

How to Evaluate a Variable

If you'll declare a variable using "let" or "var" without assigning a value, that variable will get "undefined" as its initial value.

Important Note: Accessing undeclared variables will give you an error message.

You may use undefined to check whether a variable holds a value. The image below will show you an excellent example:

```
1  var input;
2  if(input === undefined){
3    doThis();
4  } else {
5    doThat();
6  }
```

If you'll use "undefined" in the Boolean context, you'll get "false." For instance, the code below runs the function named myFunction since myArray is undefined:

```
1  var myArray = [];
2  if (!myArray[0]) myFunction();
```

The system will give you NaN if you'll use "undefined" in the Numeric context. Here's an example:

```
1  var a;
2  a + 2;  // Evaluates to NaN
```

If you'll evaluate variable that holds "null," you'll get "0" when used in the Numeric context and "false" when used in the Boolean context. Check the following example:

```
1  var n = null;
2  console.log(n * 32); // Will log 0 to the console
```

The Scope of a Variable

If you'll declare variables outside of a function, you'll get global variables. That means you can utilize such variables at any part of your JavaScript program. If in case you will declare variables inside a function, you'll get local variables. You can only use these variables through the function that holds them.

Hoisting

JavaScript allows programmers to refer to variables that haven't been declared. This technique is called variable hoisting: the system hoists (i.e. lifts to the top) variables to the top section of the statement or function. However, hoisted variables give "undefined" as their value. That means you'll still get "undefined" from a hoisted variable even after declaring and initializing it. Check the code below:

```
1   /**
2    * Example 1
3    */
4   console.log(x === undefined); // logs "true"
5   var x = 3;
6
7   /**
8    * Example 2
9    */
10  // will return a value of undefined
11  var myvar = "my value";
12
13  (function() {
14    console.log(myvar); // undefined
15    var myvar = "local value";
16  })();
```

Variable hoisting can turn your code into a confusing mess. To improve the readability and functionality of your codes, you must place your "var" statements at the top of your functions.

Global Variables

Actually, a global variable is a property of the programming environment's global object. In webpages, "window" serves as the global object. That means you may create and access a global variable through this syntax: **window.variable**.

JavaScript allows you to access variables declared within one window even if you are in a different window. You just have to specify the name of the window that holds the variables you like to access.

JavaScript Constants

As discussed above, you may use "const" to generate a read-only constant in your JavaScript programs. The rules involved in naming variables also apply to constants. You may use letters, numbers, underscores and dollar signs. However, you cannot use a number as the first character of the constant's name.

Here's an example:

const example = "69";

You cannot reassign or re-declare a constant to change its value. That means you have to be 100% sure of the data that you will assign on a constant at the time of declaration.

Additionally, you cannot create a constant with the same identifier as a variable or function within the same scope.

Data Types and Structures

In this section of the book, you'll learn about the different data types and data structures supported by JavaScript. Study this material carefully since it will provide you with important information regarding this programming language.

The Different Data Types in JavaScript

Currently, JavaScript supports seven types of data. These are:

- null – This is a keyword that denotes a null value. Since this computer language is case-sensitive, null is different from NULL, Null, and other versions of the word.

- Number – 69 or 999.99.

- Boolean – This data type has two possible values: true and false.

- String – This type of data involves letters. For example: Hello.

- undefined – This data type is considered as a top-level attribute of any program.

- Symbol – This type involves distinct and unchangeable instances.

- Object – Programmers use this data type to hold information and instructions related to the handling and usage of data.

Although small in number, these data types allow you to run cool and useful functions in your JavaScript programs. Functions and objects are two of the most basic elements of this language. You may consider objects as containers that can store information and functions as processes that your program can execute.

Converting One Data Type to Another

The JavaScript language is dynamically-typed; thus, you may declare variables without specifying the data type that they can hold. Additionally, JavaScript converts data types automatically as required during code execution. That means you can declare a variable this way:

var apple = 5;

Later, you may go back to the same variable and give it a new value. For instance:

apple = "This is delicious.";

With the codes given above, you created a variable named "apple" and gave it "5" (i.e. a number data type) as the initial value, then you replaced the number with a string (i.e. "This is delicious."). Since JavaScript is dynamically-typed, the reassignment of values won't give you an error message.

For expressions that involve string and numeric values with "+" (i.e. one of the JavaScript operators), the language converts numbers to strings. The code below will help you understand this concept:

A = "My age is " + 18 // "My age is 18"

B = 18 + " is my age" // "18 is my age"

JavaScript won't convert numbers to strings in expressions that involve other operators (e.g. -, *, /, etc.). For instance:

"69" – 9 // 60

"69" + 9 // "699"

The String-to-Number Conversion

If you used a string value to represent a number, you may convert the data type using the following functions:

- **parseFloat()**

- **parseInt()**

The **parseInt()** function returns whole numbers. That means you can use it to simplify decimal numbers. Also, it is a good programming practice to include "radix" (i.e. a parameter of the **parseInt()** function) whenever you use **parseInt()**. Basically, radix allows you to specify the numerical system that you must use.

The Literals in JavaScript

In the JavaScript language, you use a literal to represent a value. The value that we're talking about here is fixed. Aside from variables, you can also add fixed values in your JavaScript codes. In this section, you'll learn about the following kinds of literals:

- Integers

- Array Literals

- Object Literals

- Boolean Literals

- String Literals

- Floating-Point Literals

Integers

In JavaScript, you can express integers as binary, decimal, octal or hexadecimal.

- Integer literals in decimal form involve a sequence of numbers that don't accept zero as the first character.

- Octal integers use zero as their first character. As a rule, this type of integer literal can only use the following digits: 0-7.

- Hexadecimal integers begin with 0X or 0x. They can have numbers (i.e. from 0 to 9) and letters (i.e. a-f)

- Binary integers always start with 0b or 0B. They can only use two digits: 1 and 0.

Here are some examples of integer literals:

- Decimal – 1, 223 and -360

- Octal – 022, 0004 and -045

- Hexadecimal – 0x2231, 0x99111 and -0xF2A4

- Binary – 0b23, 0b1100 and -0b10

Array Literal

Basically, this type of literal is composed of 0 or more expressions. Each of these expressions represents an array object, placed inside a pair of square brackets (i.e. [ ]). If you'll generate an array through an array literal, the system will initialize it with your specified values as the objects. The length of the array is equal to the quantity of arguments you specified.

The code below creates an array called Countries with four elements and a length of four:

var Countries = ["Bulgaria", "Colombia", "Philippines", "United States of America"];

If you'll create an array through a literal inside a top-level statement, JavaScript will interpret the array every time it checks the expression that holds the array literal. Additionally, if you will use a literal for a function, the system will create that literal whenever you invoke that function.

Extra Commas inside Arrays

In JavaScript, you don't have to indicate all of the elements in an array. If you'll place two commas consecutively, the system will create the array and assign "undefined" for the objects you didn't specify. The code below creates an array called "Cars:"

var Cars = ["BMW" , , "Toyota"];

"Cars" has three elements: BMW, undefined, and Toyota.

JavaScript ignores commas that are placed at the end of the array. That means you cannot add an undefined object at the last section of your arrays.

Important Note: Trailing commas (i.e. commas that are placed at the end of arrays or statements) can produce errors in web browsers. Because of this, you should remove all of the trailing commas in your JavaScript codes.

Object Literals

Object literals are lists of an object's property names and assigned values. A pair of curly braces (i.e. {}) encloses these elements. In JavaScript, you can't place an object literal at the start of your codes. This action can result to errors and/or undesirable effects on your JavaScript programs.

The property name of an object can be any string (even an empty one). If you are using an invalid number or identifier, you must enclose it with quotation marks. To access property names that involve invalid identifiers, use a pair of brackets (i.e. [ ]).

Boolean Literals

This type involves two values: (1) true and (2) false.

Keep in mind that Boolean literals are different from the Boolean data type (which was discussed above). In general, Boolean objects serve as wrappers around the Boolean data type.

String Literals

String literals are composed of zero or more characters placed inside a pair of quotation marks (i.e. either single or double quotes). Here are some examples:

- "water"

- 'car'

- "3.14"

- "I'd like to use \t to add a tab character"

- "Peter Pan"

You may invoke any method of the string object on a string literal – JavaScript converts string literals to string objects automatically, invokes the method you need and discards the string object that was created.

Important Note: Unless your codes require string objects, you must use string literals when writing JavaScript statements.

How to Use Special Characters in your Strings

JavaScript allows you to include special characters in your strings. Here's an example:

"first line \n second line"

The table below shows the special characters supported by JavaScript:

Special Character	Purpose
\0	This character adds a null byte into your code.
\b	Using this special character is like pressing the backspace key on your keyboard.
\f	With this character, you can add a form feed into your JavaScript statements.
\n	Use this if you want to add a newline character in your codes. Typing this special character is like pressing the Enter key on your keyboard.
\r	This character allows you to apply a carriage return on your codes.
\t	This special character adds a tab character (i.e. the character you'll get after pressing the Tab key on your keyboard) into your codes.

\v	With this character, you can quickly add a vertical tab into your statements.
\'	Use this character to add an apostrophe or single quotation mark into your statements.
\"	Use this character if you want to add a double quote into your code.
\\	This character allows you to include a backslash character into your JavaScript statement.
\xxx	You can use this character to add a Latin-1 symbol to your codes. This special character requires octal digits within this range: 0-377. For instance, \251 will add "©" (i.e. the copyright symbol) into your statement.
\xXX	This is similar to the previous one. You can use this character to add Latin-1 symbols into your codes. The only difference is that this particular character requires two hexadecimal values within this range 00-FF. For instance, \xA9 adds © into your JavaScript code.
\uXXXX	This character adds Unicode symbols to your codes. It requires four hexadecimal values. For instance, \u00A9 adds © into your code.

How to Escape a Character

In JavaScript, quotation marks are used to start and terminate strings. However, in some situations, you have to include a quotation mark into your codes - that is, you want an ordinary quotation mark (not the JavaScript symbol). In this case, you must introduce the quotation mark using a backslash (i.e. \). This technique is called "escaping the character." Typing a backslash before a special symbol turns that symbol into an ordinary one.

Important Note: Sometimes, you have to add an ordinary backslash into your statements. Well, you can do that quickly and easily. You just have to type two backslashes (i.e. \\). This action "escapes" the backslash character itself.

Floating-Point Literals

Floating-point literals have the following parts:

- A decimal integer

- An exponent

- A fraction

- A decimal point

You must use "E" or "e" to represent the exponent section of your floating-point literals. After indicating the exponent, you should place the integer (which can be preceded by "-" or "+"). In general, floating-point literals should have at least one number and either an exponent or decimal point.

Here is the syntax of a floating-point literal:

```
1   [(+|-)][digits][.digits][(E|e)[(+|-)]digits]
```

Here are some examples of floating-point literals:

- .2e-34

- 3.15

- -.145

- -4.6E+69

JavaScript Keywords

This section of the book will show you all of the keywords in JavaScript. All of these words serve a special purpose in the JavaScript programming language; thus, you can't use any of them in naming your variables, functions, objects, etc.

switch	abstract	Instanceof	else
int	enum	synchronized	boolean
this	break	interface	export
long	byte	throw	extends
throws	case	native	false
new	transient	final	catch

true	class	package	char
final	null	finally	try
private	const	typeof	for
function	continue	var	protected
void	debugger	public	goto
return	default	volatile	if
implements	while	delete	short
do	with	static	import
super	double	in	

CHAPTER 3

JavaScript's Control Flow Statements

This language offers a compact group of control flow statements that you can add to your codes. In general, a control flow statement boosts the functionality and interactivity of a JavaScript program. This section of the book focuses on control flow statements.

The Block Statement

Programmers consider this as the most basic statement in JavaScript. Use this to group your JavaScript statements. When writing your programs, enclose the block statement using a pair of brackets.

The image below shows the syntax of a block statement:

```
{
    statement_1;
    statement_2;

    .

    .

    .

    statement_n;
}
```

In general, programmers use block statements for control flow statements (i.e. for, if, while, etc.). Here's an example:

while (y > 69) {

    123;

}

In the code snippet given above, "123;" serves as the block statement.

The Conditional Statements

Conditional statements are sets of commands that run if the assigned condition is true. The JavaScript language offers two kinds of conditional statements: (1) if... else and (2) switch.

Let's discuss these conditional statements in detail:

The "if... else" Statement

With this statement, you can run a command as long as the assigned condition is true. It involves an "else" clause (which is optional). The "else" clause holds a statement that will run if the assigned condition is false. The syntax of a basic "if... else" statement is:

```
if (condition) {
    statement_1;
} else {
    statement_2;
}
```

Since your condition must get either "true" or "false," you must use Boolean expressions when writing a conditional statement. If the condition is true, the first statement will run; otherwise, the second one will run.

JavaScript allows you to set multiple conditions in your conditional statements. You just have to combine several "if" and "else" clauses in a conditional statement. Here's the syntax that you must use:

```
if (condition_1) {
    statement_1;
} else if (condition_2) {
    statement_2;
} else if (condition_n) {
    statement_n;
} else {
    statement_last;
}
```

To run multiple statements, you must place them inside a block statement (i.e. { ... }). Programming experts claim that it's best to utilize block statements, particularly when combining if statements. Check the following example:

```
if (condition) {
    statement_1_runs_if_condition_is_true;
    statement_2_runs_if_condition_is_true;
} else {
    statement_3_runs_if_condition_is_false;
    statement_4_runs_if_condition_is_false;
}
```

If possible, avoid using simple assignments in your conditional expressions. This is because simple assignments are often confused with equality when checking JavaScript codes. For instance, you must not add the following code into your statements:

if (a = b) {

> **/* sample_statement */**

}

If you really need to use a simple assignment in your conditional expressions, place it between a pair of parentheses. Here's an example:

if ((x = y)) {

> **/* sample_statement */**

}

The Falsy Values

A "falsy value" is a value that evaluates to false. Here are the falsy values that you will encounter while using JavaScript:

- 0

- null

- false

- undefined

- NaN

- (" ") (i.e. an empty string)

Any value not listed above evaluates to true when used in conditional statements.

The "Switch" Statement

This kind of statement allows an application to check an expression and compare it with a predetermined set of cases. If there's a match, the application runs the assigned command. Here is the syntax of a basic switch statement:

```
switch (expression) {
    case label_1:
        statements_1
        [break;]
    case label_2:
        statements_2
        [break;]
    ...
    default:
        statements_def
        [break;]
}
```

First, the application will search for a case with a label that matches the expression's value. Then, it will pass the control flow to that particular clause, performing the assigned statement/s. If no match is found, the application will check the default clause (which is optional) and pass the control flow to that clause, running the assigned statement/s. If the statement has no default clause, the application will simply run the statement after the switch. Typically, the final clause of a switch statement serves as the default clause, but it isn't mandatory.

You may also add a break statement in your switches. A break statement makes sure that the application will get out of the switch statement once a match is found. When the application gets out of the switch, the system will run the statement right after the switch statement. If your code doesn't have a break, the application will simply run all of the commands within your switch statement.

How to Handle Exceptions

JavaScript allows you to throw and manage exceptions. To do these things, you must use the following statements:

- the "throw" statement

- the "try... catch" statement

The Different Types of Exceptions

In JavaScript, you can throw any type of object. However, thrown objects may possess different characteristics. Although it is usual to throw strings and/or numbers as error messages, it is usually more beneficial to utilize the exception types designed for this purpose. Here are two of the most popular exceptions in JavaScript:

- DOMError – This exception represents a named error object.

- DOMException - This exception indicates an abnormal situation that happens while a property or method is being used. To use this exception, you must add DOMError() into your code.

The "throw" Statement

Obviously, this statement allows you to throw exceptions. While throwing an exception, you must indicate the expression holding the data to be thrown. Here's the syntax:

```
throw expression;
```

The syntax given above can throw any type of expression. The following list shows some examples:

- **throw "Error1"; // A String type exception**

- **throw 1; // A Number type exception**

- **throw false; // A Boolean type exception**

Important Note: You may specify objects while throwing an exception. Then, you may specify the properties of the object/s inside the "catch" section of your statement.

The "try... catch" Statement

This statement looks for statement blocks that you can try. It also specifies a response that will be used in case an exception is thrown. The try... catch statement catches thrown exceptions.

Try... catch statements have three parts, which are:

1. The "try" section – It holds one or more JavaScript statements. This part is mandatory.

2. The "catch" section – This part holds statements that indicate what the program must do in case an exception gets thrown. That means if the "try" section doesn't succeed, the program control will go to the "catch" section. If a statement inside the "try" section throws an exception, the program control will immediately go to the catch section. If no exceptions arise, however, the system will skip the statement's catch section.

   In JavaScript, you may use the catch section to manage all exceptions that may be thrown in the try section. Here's the syntax that you should use:

```
catch (catchID) {
    statements
}
```

In the syntax given above, "catchID" represents the identifier that contains the value assigned in your throw statement. You may employ this identifier to acquire data regarding the thrown exception/s. JavaScript generates this identifier whenever the catch section executes. The identifier lasts only while the catch section is active. That means the identifier will cease to exist once the catch section has finished its execution.

For instance, the code below generates an exception. Once the exception is thrown, program control will go to the catch section.

```
1  try {
2      throw "myException"; // generates an exception
3  }
4  catch (e) {
5      // statements to handle any exceptions
6      logMyErrors(e); // pass exception object to error handler
7  }
```

Important Note: This section is completely optional.

3. The "finally" section – It holds statements that will run after executing the previous sections. The statements placed inside the "finally" section will run whether or

not the program encountered an exception. Additionally, statements within this section will still run even if the statement has no "catch" section.

In general, programmers use this section to set graceful exits for their projects whenever an exception happens. For instance, they may need to liberate some resources that are affected by the problematic script. The image below will help you understand how this section works.

```
1   openMyFile();
2   try {
3       writeMyFile(theData); //This may throw a error
4   } catch(e) {
5       handleError(e); // If we got a error we handle it
6   } finally {
7       closeMyFile(); // always close the resource
8   }
```

With the code given above, JavaScript opens a file and runs statements that utilize the file. If JavaScript encounters an error, the "finally" section will close the file before the whole code terminates.

How to Utilize an Error Object

In some cases, you may get more information about an error by checking its properties (i.e. its 'name' and 'message'). This functionality is extremely useful if your code's catch section doesn't indicate whether errors are generated by the user or the system itself. To utilize error objects, you have to use a JavaScript tool called "Error Constructor." Here's an example:

```
1   function doSomethingErrorProne () {
2     if (ourCodeMakesAMistake()) {
3       throw (new Error('The message'));
4     } else {
5       doSomethingToGetAJavascriptError();
6     }
7   }
8   ....
9   try {
10    doSomethingErrorProne();
11  }
12  catch (e) {
13    console.log(e.name); // logs 'Error'
14    console.log(e.message); // logs 'The message' or a JavaScript error
15  }
```

JavaScript Promises

The JavaScript language now supports "promises" (i.e. an object that allows programmers to manage the flow of delayed and asynchronous processes).

Promises undergo the following states:

- Pending – This is the initial status of a promise. In this state, a promise may get rejected or fulfilled.

- Fulfilled – A promise becomes "fulfilled" if the system successfully completes all of the assigned processes.

- Settled – A settled promise can be either rejected or fulfilled.

- Rejected – In a rejected promise, the system failed to complete the assigned processes.

CHAPTER 4

The Different Types of Loops in JavaScript

A loop allows you to repeat code snippets quickly and easily. This chapter will concentrate on the different kinds of loops offered by JavaScript.

General Information

While writing your own codes, you'll find situations where you have to use the same codes over and over again. This kind of task is boring and time-consuming. However, you can't skip it since your application won't work properly without the proper codes.

Fortunately, JavaScript supports loop statements. A loop statement allows you to repeat code blocks automatically. That means you won't have to spend much time and effort in completing your JavaScript codes.

Loops are designed to repeat codes. They have different mechanisms that can be adjusted to improve their effectiveness in copying codes. Additionally, each loop type has distinct characteristics that make them extremely useful and convenient in certain situations. Here are the loop statements that you'll find in JavaScript:

- "for"

- "while"

- "do... while"

- "label"

- "break"

- "for... of"

- "for... in"

- "continue"

The "for" Loop

Basically, "for" loops repeat a statement until an assigned condition results to false. The syntax of JavaScript "for" loops is similar to that of C and Java. Here's the syntax:

```
for ([initialExpression]; [condition]; [incrementExpression])
  statement
```

The following things happen whenever a "for" loop runs:

1. The loop's initializing expression (represented by initialExpression in the syntax above) performs its function/s. Often, an initializing expression triggers multiple loop counters. That means the syntax given above accepts different levels of complexity. You may

also use this expression to declare variables.

Important Note: The initializing expression is optional; thus, you can create effective "for" loops without using any initializing expression.

2. The system evaluates the conditional expression. If the evaluation is true, the statements contained in the loop will run. However, if the evaluation is false, the entire loop will stop.

Important Note: The conditional expression is optional. If you won't add a conditional expression in your "for" loop, the system will assume that the evaluation is true.

3. The statement runs. If you want to run multiple statements, you must group them into a block (i.e. by enclosing them in curly braces).

4. The final expression (represented by incrementExpression in the syntax) updates the entire loop, then the control flow will go back to the second step (see above).

The "while" Loop

"While" loops execute their statement/s while the assigned condition results to "true." Here is the syntax of a "while" loop:

```
while (condition)
    statement
```

Once the condition results to "false", the loop will stop running the assignments assigned to it, then the control flow will go to the statement right after the "while" loop.

The system evaluates the condition prior to running the loop itself. If the condition is true, the statement/s inside the loop will run and the system will check the condition again. If the condition is false, the loop will stop and the control flow will move on to the next statement.

Important Note: Since the condition test happens first, a "while" loop may never run. That means you have to be extremely careful when creating "while" loops in your JavaScript programs.

JavaScript allows you to enclose multiple statements using a pair of curly braces. Use this option if you want to include various statements in your "while" loops.

The "do... while" Loop

This kind of loop runs its statement/s until the assigned condition becomes false. When creating a "do... while" loop, you must use the following syntax:

```
do
    statement
while (condition);
```

Here, the system executes the statements once before checking the assigned condition. If the condition is true, the system will execute the statements again. This process will continue until the condition becomes false. Once the condition evaluates to false, the control flow will go to the statement right after the "do... while" loop.

In this type of loop, the statements are guaranteed to run at least once even if the condition is false.

The "label" Statement

This kind of statement allows you to "label" (i.e. assign an identifier) your statements. By labeling your JavaScript statements, you can easily repeat them at any part of your application. For instance, you may label a certain loop, and utilize other statements to either continue or disrupt its execution.

Here is the syntax of a "label" statement:

```
label :
    statement
```

When creating a label, you may use any identifier that isn't a JavaScript keyword. You may use the syntax given above for any statement.

The "break" Statement

Programmers use this statement to end loop or switch statements. When using a "break" statement, you must remember the following rules:

- If your break statement doesn't have a label, it will terminate the innermost loop/switch and pass the control flow to the next statement.

- If your break statement has a label, it will terminate the labeled statement.

The syntax of a break statement is:

```
1. break;

2. break label;
```

Use the first variant of the syntax if you don't need to specify a label. This will terminate the innermost loop/switch. Use the second variant if you want to terminate a certain loop/switch. Just enter the label of that particular loop or switch. When using the second variant, only the specified loop/switch will be terminated.

The "for... of" Statement

This statement is a recent addition to the JavaScript language. It creates a loop that can repeat "iterable objects" (e.g. maps, sets, arrays, arguments, etc.). It also invokes an iteration hook that will run for each distinct property of an object. JavaScript allows you to customize the iteration hook of any "for... of" statement. Here is the syntax that you must use:

```
for (variable of object) {
    statement
}
```

The "for... in" Statement

A "for... in" statement repeats the assigned statement/s over the properties of any object. JavaScript will execute the assigned statement/s for every property. The syntax of a "for... in" statement is:

```
for (variable in object) {
    statements
}
```

The "continue" Statement

You may use this statement to restart other statements (e.g. for, while, do... while, and label). Here are the two rules that you must remember when using a "continue" statement:

- If you won't include a label in your continue statement, it will terminate the current process of the innermost loop and continue the next one. Unlike a break statement, a continue statement cannot terminate an entire loop. If used on "while" loops, the control flow will return to the assigned condition. If used on a "for" loop, on the other hand, the control flow will go back to the increment expression.

- If you'll include a label in your continue statement, it will only affect the statement linked to that label.

The syntax of a continue statement has two forms, which are:

1. `continue;`

2. `continue label;`

CHAPTER 5

JavaScript Functions

In general, functions serve as "subprograms" that you can invoke using internal/external codes. Similar to a complete program, a function has a group of statements known as its "body." JavaScript allows you to pass values to a function. Additionally, a function can return a value.

JavaScript considers functions as first-class objects, since they possess methods and properties found in other programming objects. The main difference between functions and other JavaScript objects is that you can invoke a function whenever you need to.

What is a Function?

In JavaScript, each function is treated as a unique object. Also, functions are different from procedures. Functions return a value 100% of the time, while some procedures don't.

You must add a "return" statement in your functions if you want them to return a value. The "return" statement specifies the value/s that must be returned. Functions that don't have a return statement give a default value. In most cases, the default value of a function is "undefined."

The arguments of a function are the parameters used in calling it. JavaScript uses values to pass arguments to a function. If a function modifies an argument's value, the modification won't appear globally or inside the function itself. However, an object reference is a value too (and a special one at that) – if a function alters the properties of a referred object, the alteration/s will appear globally.

How to Define a Function

In JavaScript, you can define functions in different ways. Let's discuss each approach in detail:

- Using the function statement – JavaScript offers a special syntax that you can use to declare a function. The syntax is:

```
function name([param[, param[, ... param]]]) {
    statements
}
```

That syntax has three different parts, which are:

- o name – This is the name of the function. You may replace this with any valid identifier.

- o param – This is the argument/parameter that you want to pass to the function. JavaScript allows you to include up to 255 parameters in each function.

- o statements – This section holds the statements (i.e. the body) of a function.

52

- Through the function expression – This approach is similar to the previous one. In fact, it uses the syntax (see below):

```
function [name]([param[, param[, ... param]]]) {
    statements
}
```

- Using JavaScript's "Function Constructor" – JavaScript allows you to generate functions using "new" (i.e. a JavaScript operator). Here is the syntax that you must use:

```
new Function (arg1, arg2, ... argN, functionBody)
```

The syntax given above has the following parts:

- o arg1, arg2, ... argN – This part holds the name/s you want to use as the formal parameter/s.

- o functionBody – This is a string that holds JavaScript statements (i.e. the body of the function).

How to Call a Function

When defining a function, you are just naming that function and assigning what to be done once the function is invoked/called. Call a function if you want it to perform the assigned actions.

For instance, if you have defined the "square" function, you may call it using the following code:

square(2);

The code given above calls the "square" function and assigns 2 as the argument. The function runs its statements and gives 4 as the resulting value.

Your functions must be within the proper scope when you call them. However, you can hoist (i.e. lift to the top) your function declarations. Here's an example:

```
1  console.log(square(5));
2  /* ... */
3  function square(n) { return n*n }
```

A function's arguments may hold different programming elements (i.e. not just numbers and strings). JavaScript allows you to assign entire objects to your functions. For example, **show_props()** (i.e. a built-in JavaScript function) accepts objects as arguments.

The Scope of a Function

If you defined a variable within a function, you won't be able to access that variable from outside the function. That's because you defined the variable within the function's scope only. A function, however, can access all of the variables and other functions created within the scope in which it was defined. Simply put, global functions can access global variables. A nested function (i.e. a function placed inside another function) can access the variables created inside its "mother function."

The Arguments of a Function

JavaScript treats arguments as array objects. Inside a function, you may access the arguments it contains using the following syntax:

arguments[n]

In this syntax, "n" represents the argument's ordinal number, beginning at zero. That means the initial argument of a function is arguments[0].

If you'll use the JavaScript object called "arguments," you may invoke functions that hold more arguments than what was declared in the code. This object can be extremely useful, especially if you have no idea about the number of arguments that you must assign to a function. To determine the quantity of objects inside a function, you may use **arguments.length**. Then, you may use the "arguments" object to access the function's arguments.

The Parameters of a Function

Currently, JavaScript supports two types of parameters: default and rest.

The Default Parameters

In the JavaScript language, the default parameter of any function is "undefined." In most situations, however, it is beneficial to change this default value. The default parameters can help you in this regard.

Before, the usual approach for setting a default value was to check parameter values inside the function's body and assign a new value if the system shows "undefined." With the default parameters, you won't have to check the function's body anymore. You may just assign numbers or strings as the new default value of your functions.

The Rest Parameters

This kind of parameter allows you to represent any number of arguments as a simple array. In the code below, you'll use rest parameters to get the second, third and fourth arguments. You can then multiply them using the first argument.

```
1  function multiply(multiplier, ...theArgs) {
2     return theArgs.map(x => multiplier * x);
3  }
4
5  var arr = multiply(2, 1, 2, 3);
6  console.log(arr); // [2, 4, 6]
```

CHAPTER 6

Events

Events – The Basics

Whenever the user or the browser controls a webpage, JavaScript codes interact with HTML content. The system handles these interactions as events.

Basically, the term "event" refers to any manipulation done on a webpage (e.g. clicking on a button, resizing the webpage, pressing a key, closing a pop-up window, etc.).

As a JavaScript programmer, you may use events to run certain responses (e.g. closing a window, displaying a message, validating records, etc.).

Events belong to DOM (Document Object Model) Level 3. Additionally, each HTML element holds a collection of events that can initiate JavaScript codes.

This chapter will discuss some of the most popular webpage events. This material will help you to understand the relationship between events and the JavaScript language.

The "onclick" Event

JavaScript users encounter this kind of event frequently. Basically, an "onclick" event happens whenever a user clicks the left-side button of his mouse. You may link warnings, validations and other content to this event.

Here's an example:

```html
<html>
<head>
<script type="text/javascript">
<!--
function sayHello() {
    document.write ("Hello World")
}
//-->
</script>
</head>
<body>
<p> Click the following button and see result</p>
<input type="button" onclick="sayHello()" value="Say Hello" />
</body>
</html>
```

If you'll run that code, you will get the following output:

Click the following button and see result

Say Hello

The "onsubmit" Event

This event happens whenever a user submits a form. Typically, programmers link their form validations to this kind of event.

The "onmouseout" and "onmouseover" Events

These two kinds of events can help you add cool effects (e.g. text, images, etc.) into your HTML documents. Basically, "onmouseout" runs once the user moves the mouse out of an element. On the other hand, "onmouseover" runs once the user brings the mouse over an element.

The Standard Events in HTML 5

The following table shows the standard events supported by HTML 5.

Attribute	Explanation
onblur	This event happens whenever a window loses focus.
Offline	This event occurs when the HTML file becomes offline.
oncanplay	It happens when a playable media is present. The playable media might need to stop because of buffering.
onabort	It occurs during an abort situation.
onbeforeprint	This event occurs before the system prints the HTML document.
onafterprint	This event happens once system has printed the HTML document.

onclick	It happens once the user clicks the left-side button of his mouse.
ondblclick	This event occurs when the user double-clicks the left-side button of his mouse.
ondrag	It happens when the user drags an HTML element.
onchange	It occurs when an HTML element changes.
ondragend	It happens once the user stops dragging an HTML element.
onmouseup	This event occurs whenever the user releases a mouse button.
onmousewheel	It happens when the user rotates the wheel of his mouse.
onpagehide	This event happens when the user hides
onredo	This occurs when the user conducts a redo on the HTML document.
onstorage	This event occurs whenever an HTML file loads.
onmessage	It occurs whenever the user triggers the assigned message.
onmousedown	This event happens whenever the user presses a mouse button.
ononline	This event occurs when the HTML file becomes online.

CHAPTER 7

JavaScript and Cookies

What is a Cookie?

Web servers and browsers utilize HTTP to communicate. However, the HTTP protocol is stateless (i.e. it treats requests as independent transactions). That means that the system won't remember any of the previous transactions. This can be a huge problem for commercial sites, since they need to share the user's information across various webpages.

In most cases, cookies help websites in tracking and remembering transactions; thus, cookies can help you improve the user-friendliness and overall traffic of your website.

How Does a Cookie Work?

The web server sends information to the user's internet browser as a cookie. If the browser accepts the cookie, the information will be converted to plaintext inside the user's hard drive. Once the user visits another webpage on your site, his browser will send the same cookie to the web server for data retrieval. Once data has been retrieved, your web server will know what has occurred before.

Basically, a cookie is a plaintext data record that has 5 fields (which are variable-length). These fields are:

- Domain – This is your website's domain name.

- Secure – If this field is tagged as "secure," only a secure webserver can retrieve the cookie. If it is blank, however, any webserver can access the cookie.

- Expires – This field specifies the date at which the cookie will expire. If this field is blank, the cookie will expire as soon the user closes the web browser.

- Path – This is the path to the webpage or directory that created the cookie. If you want to retrieve cookies from any page or directory, you may leave this field empty.

- Name=Value – Each cookie is set and retrieved as key-value pairs.

Cookies were created for CGI (i.e. Common Gateway Interface) programming. The information stored in a cookie is transmitted automatically between the webserver and the user's web browser. That means CGI scripts written on the webserver can read and edit cookie information stored on the user's hard drive.

JavaScript allows you to manage cookies using the **Document** object's **cookie** property. The JavaScript language can create, read, alter, and delete cookies that are applied on the active webpage.

How to Create a Cookie?

The easiest way to generate a cookie is to place a string value to the object named document.cookie. The syntax that you should use is:

```
document.cookie = "key1=value1;key2=value2;expires=date";
```

In this syntax, **expires** is completely optional. If you'll enter a valid time or date on this field, the cookie will expire on that particular time or date. You won't be able to access the values stored in an expired cookie.

Important Note: You can't save whitespaces, commas, or semicolons into a cookie. Thus, you have to encode those characters using the **escape()** function before saving them onto a cookie. If you'll encode characters this way, you should also use **unescape()** to allow the system to read the value you stored.

How to Read a Cookie

You can read cookies easily. This is because the cookie is the value stored on the object named "document.cookie". That means you can use that string to access the cookie whenever you want. Basically, document.cookie contains a set of name=value pairs that are separated by semicolons. Here, **name** is the cookie's name and **value** is the cookie's string value.

How to Set a Cookie's Expiry Date

In some cases, you have to extend the cookie's life beyond the current browsing session. By doing so, you can complete long processes without having to reenter any piece of information. JavaScript allows you to set your preferred expiration date and save that information inside the cookie itself. You can accomplish this by customizing the cookie's "expires" attribute.

The image below shows you how to set a cookie's expiration date. It extends the current expiry date by one month.

```html
<html>
<head>
<script type="text/javascript">
<!--
function WriteCookie()
{
    var now = new Date();
    now.setMonth( now.getMonth() + 1 );
    cookievalue = escape(document.myform.customer.value) + ";"
    document.cookie="name=" + cookievalue;
    document.cookie = "expires=" + now.toUTCString() + ";"
    document.write ("Setting Cookies : " + "name=" + cookievalue );
}
//-->
</script>
</head>
<body>
<form name="formname" action="">
Enter name: <input type="text" name="customer"/>
<input type="button" value="Set Cookie" onclick="WriteCookie()"/>
</form>
</body>
</html>
```

How to Delete a Cookie

In most cases, you must delete cookies after using them. This ensures that the webserver won't get any information from the unnecessary cookie. Deleting a cookie is easy and simple. You just have to set the expiration date to a time in the past.

CHAPTER 8

Page Redirection

Page Redirection – The Basics

You have probably tried to access a certain webpage but you were redirected to a different one. That event occurs because of page redirection. Don't confuse this with Page Refresh (which will be discussed below).

There are lots of reasons why you'd need to redirect users from a certain page. Here are the most common reasons:

- You are transferring your website to a new domain name. In this case, you need to forward all of your website traffic to the new domain. You don't have to delete the old website. You can keep it and use page redirection to get all the web traffic. This approach can help you keep your previous customers who may not be aware of your new site.

- You created webpages based on certain criteria (e.g. browser types, the customers' name, the country where the customer resides, etc.). Rather than redirecting visitors through server-side mechanisms, you may employ client-side redirection to forward your visitors to the correct webpage.

- You want to retain the traffic from your old SEO campaign even though you have switched to a new website. Search engines may ban your website from their search results pages if you'll use page redirection to get illegal web traffic.

Page Refresh

In JavaScript, you may refresh webpages using the **location. reload** method. You can call this method automatically or when a user clicks on a certain link. If you like to refresh a webpage based on mouse clicks, you should use the code below:

```
<a href="javascript:location.reload(true)">Refresh Page</a>
```

Automatic Refresh

JavaScript allows you to refresh a webpage after a certain amount of time. You just have to use **setTimeout()** (i.e. a pre-installed JavaScript function) to run a different function after a predetermined time interval.

How Does Page Redirection Work?

Programmers implement page redirection in different ways. Here are some examples:

1. You may use JavaScript to implement a client-side page redirection. To forward your website visitors to the new

webpage, you just have to add a line in your HTML document's head section. Here's an example:

```
<html>
<head>
<script type="text/javascript">
<!--
function Redirect() {
    window.location="http://www.tutorialspoint.com";
}
//-->
</script>
</head>
<body>
<p>Click the following button, you will be redirected to home page.</p>
<form>
<input type="button" value="Redirect Me" onclick="Redirect();" />
</form>
</body>
</html>
```

2. You may display a message to your website visitors before forwarding them to the new webpage. This approach involves a delay: the old webpage has to load the message you want to show. The code below will show you how to use this approach using the JavaScript language.

```
<html>
<head>
<script type="text/javascript">
<!--
function Redirect() {
    window.location="http://www.tutorialspoint.com";
}
document.write ("You will be redirected to our main page in 10
seconds!");
setTimeout('Redirect()', 10000);
//-->
</script>
</head>
<body>
</body>
</html>
```

3. You may redirect users based on the browser that they are using. The following example will show you how it's done:

```html
<html>
<head>
<script type="text/javascript">
<!--
var browsername=navigator.appName;
if( browsername == "Netscape" )
{
    window.location="http://www.location.com/ns.htm";
}
else if ( browsername =="Microsoft Internet Explorer")
{
    window.location="http://www.location.com/ie.htm";
}
else
{
    window.location="http://www.location.com/other.htm";
}
//-->
</script>
</head>
<body>
</body>
</html>
```

CHAPTER 9

Dialog Boxes

The JavaScript language supports three kinds of dialog boxes. You may use these dialog boxes to raise an alert, confirm any input, or ask users to enter certain pieces of information. This chapter will discuss each type of dialog box in detail.

The Alert Box

Use this box to display a warning message for your website visitors. For instance, if the user doesn't enter any input in a mandatory field, you may use an alert dialog box to warn that user. Programmers consider this kind of dialog box as an important part of user validation.

Important Note: You may also use an alert box to display friendly messages. Also, an alert box has a single button (i.e. the "OK" button). The user needs to click on the button before he/she can proceed.

The Confirmation Box

In general, you'll use this dialog box to ask for the user's consent. This dialog box has two buttons: OK and Quit (or Cancel).

Website developers use this dialog box to confirm the visitor's intention to proceed with an action. You'll see confirmation boxes on adult websites and those that require confidential information.

The Prompt Box

This dialog box is extremely useful if you need to display a text box that can accept user input. That means you can use a prompt box to interact with your website visitors. Your visitors have to enter the required information and hit the OK button.

To display a prompt dialog box on a webpage, you must use the **prompt()** method. This method accepts two parameters: (1) the label that you want to show in the dialog box and (2) the text string that you want to show in the dialog box.

Similar to a confirmation box, a prompt box has an OK button and a Quit/Cancel button. If the website visitor hits OK, the **prompt()** method will submit the data entered in the text box. If the visitor hits Quit/Cancel, on the other hand, the **prompt()** method will submit **null** to the webserver

CHAPTER 10

How to Use the Void Keyword

The "void" keyword plays an important part in the JavaScript language. You can use "void" as a unary operator (i.e. an operator that works on a single operand) for any kind of operand. Basically, "void" identifies the expression to be checked without giving any value.

The Syntax

The syntax of this keyword has two forms:

1.
```
<head>
<script type="text/javascript">
<!--
void func()
javascript:void func()
```

2.
```
void(func())
javascript:void(func())
//-->
</script>
</head>
```

To help you understand this keyword, let's analyze two practical examples:

- Programmers often use this keyword in the client-side form of JavaScript. For example, they can use "void" on a URL to get the side-effects of an expression without showing the result on the web browser.

- Analyze the code below. The link it contains won't do anything since the expression "0" is meaningless in the JavaScript language. JavaScript evaluates "0" but it doesn't load the expression into the HTML document.

```html
<html>
<head>
<script type="text/javascript">
<!--
//-->
</script>
</head>
<body>
<p>Click the following, This won't react at all...</p>
<a href="javascript:void(0)">Click me!</a>
</body>
</html>
```

CHAPTER 11

Debugging

Programmers are humans – they make mistakes every now and then. Mistakes in a script or a program are called "bugs."

The act of searching for and resolving bugs is known as "debugging." Programmers consider debugging as an important aspect of the development procedure. This chapter will discuss the tools and methods that you can use to perform debugging tasks.

The Error Messages in Internet Explorer

The simplest approach to find errors is by activating the "Error Information" option of a web browser. Internet Explorer, for instance, displays an icon in its status bar whenever an error occurs on a webpage. Here's a screenshot:

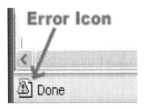

If you'll double-click on that icon, Internet Explorer will display a dialog box containing details about the error it encountered.

Since you can easily overlook this icon, Internet Explorer allows you to set the system so that it will display the error dialog box each time an error happens. To turn on that option, just click on "Tools" and hit "Internet Options". Click on the tab named "Advanced" and put a check on the box that says: "Display a Notification about Every Script Error."

Here's a screenshot:

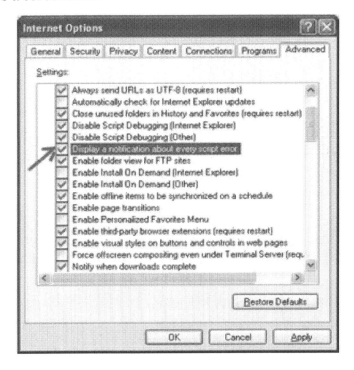

The Error Messages in Netscape and Firefox

Netscape and Firefox send error details to a window named "Error Console" or "JavaScript Console." You can view this window by clicking on "Tools" and selecting "Error Console."

However, because these two browsers don't have an error icon, you have to keep the Error Console open as you execute your

JavaScript codes.

The Error Notifications

The error notifications that you see on your browser (e.g. Internet Explorer, Netscape, Firefox, etc.) are caused by runtime and syntax errors. These notifications contain detailed information (e.g. line numbers) regarding the error. That means you can use these error notifications to find and solve errors quickly.

If you are using Mozilla Firefox, you may click on the errors listed in the Console to check the exact line that caused the problem.

Debugging your Scripts

JavaScript offers a powerful approach in debugging a script:

Using a validator – In JavaScript, you may use a validator to ensure that your codes follow the syntax rules of this language. Validators (also known as validating passers) usually come with premium JavaScript and HTML editors.

JavaScript Lint, which was developed by Douglas Crockford, is one of the leading validators today. You can use it for free here: http://www.jslint.com/

Just access that webpage, paste the JavaScript code onto the editing area, and hit the button that says "JSLint." This computer program will analyze your code, making sure that each of its parts follows the right syntax.

Conclusion

Thank you for reading this book!

I hope this book was able to teach you the basics of JavaScript.

The next step is to write your own webpages and applications using the JavaScript programming language.

Would you do me a favor?

Finally, if you enjoyed this book, please take the time to share your thoughts and post a positive review on Amazon. It'd be greatly appreciated!

Thank you and good luck!

Made in the USA
San Bernardino, CA
05 February 2016